CONTENTS

INTRODUCTION

Since the second book of the Bible, *Exodus*, is the basis of this booklet, I would like to show its importance for us as Christians. In the words of Peter Ellis, ". . . the basic importance of *Exodus* lies in the fact that it gives us the blueprint of the Kingdom of God, the basic plan upon which the Church instituted by Christ is built. It is important also because of its use in the liturgy: in the Holy Week services, in the prayers at baptism, in the Mass and Office during the paschal season. This use is prompted by the abundance of types found in *Exodus*, outlining in a veiled manner the history of our redemption wrought by Christ.

"The basic parallelism of the types may be summed up as follows: as Moses led the Israelites* from captivity in Egypt, through the Red Sea to a new life as God's redeemed, and from the sea to the promised land, directed

---

*Israelites: the Chosen People of God in the Old Testament, also referred to as Israel.

by a pillar of fire, fed by miraculous bread (manna) and miraculous meat (quail) and water from a rock . . . so Christ, the new Moses, the paschal lamb, sacrificed on Mt. Calvary, leads his Chosen People through the Red Sea of his redeeming Blood, by baptism, to the new Christian life in which, leading the life of the resurrected Christ, the redeemed follow Christ, the light of the world, through this life as a desert, eating his flesh, drinking his blood, until they ascend with him into the Promised Land, the kingdom of heaven. When engaged in liturgical prayer, the worshiper should go immediately from the types to the anti-types. St. Paul in 1 Cor. 10:1-13 is an excellent guide on how to read *Exodus* and *Numbers*.

"Finally, *Exodus* is most important for an understanding of the rest of the Bible. Future inspired writers, prophets, historians, evangelists, look back upon these events, draw comparisons and make innumerable allusions. No one can read the prophets and the wisdom writers nor even much of the Gospels and St. Paul with real appreciation and understanding unless he has read and digested the great theological impact of the *Exodus* and the Sinai covenant.

"In conclusion, we can say that the theme of *Exodus* is the story of the greatest event in the whole history of the Chosen People: its sublime elevation to the dignity of a theocratic nation, directed, ruled, and protected by the one true God. The book gives the foundation of this kingdom, its laws and regulations, some of its vicissitudes. It ends with the construction and dedication of the Ark and the Tabernacle, in which from this time on, God will dwell in the midst of his people. This last event is by no means something loosely related to the covenant, but rather its immediate consequence and its glorious consummation. With the dedication of the Tabernacle and God's coming to dwell there, the Kingdom of God on earth begins. In a similar manner, twelve hundred and fifty years later, God dedicates the tabernacle of Mary's body, and at the annunciation his only-begotten Son takes his place there to fulfill the promise made to Abraham, becoming no longer the "expected" but the arrived "blessing of all nations," in whose Mystical Body all men are called to salvation" (*The Men and the Message of the Old Testament*, pp. 33-34).

Every possible preparation was made that the Jewish people would understand the meaning of the Passover celebration. It was expounded for a month in the synagogue, and it was taught daily in the schools. Every effort was made that no one would come ignorant or be unprepared for the celebration.

How prepared are we to participate intelligently and fruitfully in the Holy Week services and in the Mass? Without understanding the Old Covenant,* we cannot have a deeper appreciation of the Holy Week services and the Mass. The purpose of this booklet is to help provide this understanding.

---

*Covenant: a special relationship of God with his people; a pact, an agreement.

Since probably most of us are acquainted more with the third chapter than with the first two chapters, one can very beneficially begin this booklet with the third chapter. However, even the third and the fourth chapters, taken by themselves, will prove very enlightening and enriching. Since we will be celebrating the Eucharist* for the rest of our lives, the reading and re-reading of this booklet, especially around the paschal season, will make the Eucharist more meaningful for us and become truly the source, center and summit of our Christian life.

---

*Today, the use of the term *Eucharist* is preferred to the word *Mass*. Here they will be used interchangeably.

Chapter One

THE OLD COVENANT*

FALL OF FIRST PARENTS

From all eternity God willed to create us and to share with us his own love and divine life. He created Adam and Eve in his image and likeness and gave them a share in his divine life. Through them and with their collaboration, God wanted to establish and develop his kingdom on earth, a kingdom which would be fully realized in heaven. But, unfortunately, Adam and Eve did

---

*To have a deeper appreciation of this section, the reader is encouraged to read *Exodus* in its entirety.

not cooperate with God's plan. Their sin of disobedience separated us from God and delayed God's plan for establishing his kingdom. We all know and experience the punishment of their sin. However, God's love for us was so great that he promised a redeemer, who would bring about a reconciliation with God.

ABRAHAM

For many, long centuries there was no indication that God was doing anything about sending a redeemer. But God is always faithful to his promises. About 1850 B.C., God revealed himself to Abram and invited him to leave his country and prosperous life and go where God would direct him. Because of Abram's willing obedience, God made a covenant with him: Abram would become the father of a new nation, out of which would come the promised redeemer, and God would be the God of Abram and his descendants. Abram would be like a tiny mustard seed from which would grow a great nation. With Abram, God would form the ethnic group which would be the beginning of God's kingdom on earth. The sign of this covenant was twofold: 1) a change of name and 2) circumcision. God changed Abram's name to Abraham, and he required that Abraham and his descendants be circumcised. The new name and circumcision would be the sign of their being sons of Abraham and sharers in the covenant. Later on, God renewed the covenant with Isaac, Jacob, and others.

ISRAELITES IN EGYPT

About seventeen centuries before Christ, Jacob's household, numbering about seventy people, was driven by famine into Egypt. For a very long time, the Israelites lived well and at peace in Egypt, and they grew from a small family into a numerous people. About 1500 B.C., the Egyptians threw off the yoke of the Hyksos who had oppressed them since 1760 B.C. Since the Egyptians disliked the Israelites and feared them because of their growing number and strength, the Israelites were soon

---

OLD COVENANT

Moses freed the Israelites from the bondage of the Egyptians

NEW COVENANT

Jesus freed us from the bondage of the devil and sin

---

oppressed and enslaved. For over two hundred years they lived in bondage, were cruelly persecuted, and were forced into slave-labor. Cries of pain, hunger, thirst, persecution, and oppression were frequent. Some of God's people, however, never lost faith completely; they increased their prayers for deliverance. Undoubtedly, God permitted them to suffer so long because suffering unites people and makes them realize their dependence upon him. God's plan required a united people, and they were far from being united.

11

MOSES

Finally, when he deemed it opportune, God answered the people's cries for deliverance. Moses, to whom God appeared in a burning bush, was to be his instrument. God sent him to the Pharaoh of Egypt with the command that the Pharaoh should let the Israelites go free. He was given miraculous powers to convince him that he came from God. The nine plagues predicted

---

OLD COVENANT

The Israelites were saved by the blood of a paschal lamb

NEW COVENANT

We were saved by the blood of the paschal lamb, Jesus

---

by Moses (water changed into blood, frogs, mosquitoes, flies, death of livestock, boils, hail, locusts, and three days of darkness) afflicted only the Egyptians, not the Israelites. By witnessing these plagues, the Israelites were convinced that God was present and active among them. But Pharaoh was adamant; he would not let the people go free. Not until after the tenth plague, the death of the first-born of the Egyptians, would the Israelites be freed.

PASSOVER-EXODUS

To be spared this plague, the Israelites were to kill an unblemished male lamb. Its bones were not to be broken, its flesh was to be eaten, and its blood was to be smeared on the outside of their house above the door and on the doorposts. This having been done, the angel of death would pass during the night throughout all of Egypt and take the life of every first-born male; but when the angel of death would see the blood around the doors of the Israelites, he would "pass-over" their houses, and their first-born would be spared.

OLD COVENANT

The angel of death "passed over" the houses of the Israelites

NEW COVENANT

Jesus had undergone a "passover" to save us

During that night, not one Egyptian house was without its dead. Since there was so much grief and wailing throughout Egypt, Pharaoh summoned Moses and told him to take his people and depart from Egypt. By the blood of the "passover lamb" they were saved from death and freed from Egyptian slavery; by the flesh of the "passover lamb" they were nourished for the beginning of the long journey toward the Promised Land. This took place about 1270 B.C.

With great joy, the people began their exodus from Egypt. Throughout their journey, God was visibly with them, by night in the form of a pillar of fire to give them light, by day in the form of a cloud to show them the way and to hide them from their enemies. In the meantime, Pharaoh realized the mistake he had made in setting the Israelites free, for there would be no one to do the work of these slaves he had set free. So he ordered his troops to ride out in their chariots and bring back the Israelites. Coming to the bank of the Red Sea, and seeing the Egyptian troops riding toward them from behind, the terrified Israelites cried out against Moses for bringing them into the wilderness to die, either by drowning or at the hands of the soldiers.

OLD COVENANT

The Israelites "passed over" from the land of slavery to the land of freedom through the Red Sea

NEW COVENANT

We "passed over" from slavery to sin and self to freedom in God through Baptism

---

Moses told the people not to fear because God would save them again. At the command of God, Moses raised his staff and stretched out his hand over the sea. The water parted and the people walked over to the other side. The charioteers followed, and when they were all in the sea, God told Moses to stretch out his hand over the sea again. The water flowed back and all the Egyptians were drowned. Again, Israel "passed-over" from certain capture and slavery to freedom. The people's faith in God and Moses was strengthened.

MOUNT SINAI AND THE COVENANT

Several months after leaving Egypt, the Israelites encamped at the foot of Mt. Sinai. Here took place a central event in the history of the Israelites: the covenant which God made with them. Since God rescued the Israelites from Egypt, there was a special relationship between them and God, and this relationship was cemented with the covenant. Because of this covenant God would be with them, take care of them, guide them,

---

OLD COVENANT

God made a covenant with the Israelites at Mount Sinai

NEW COVENANT

Jesus made a new covenant with us at the Last Supper

---

and give them their own country. They in turn would have to recognize their dependence upon him and obey his laws. As God expressed it: "You yourselves have seen what I did with the Egyptians, how I carried you on eagle's wings and brought you to myself. From this you know that now, if you obey my voice and hold fast my covenant, you of all nations shall be my very own for all the earth is mine. I will count you a kingdom of priests, a consecrated nation" (Ex. 19:4-6).

This covenant formed them into a community, a People of God. The Ten Commandments and other laws

15

given to them by God were their charter as a nation. The people agreed to obey all of God's laws: "We will observe all that Yahweh has decreed; we will obey" (Ex. 24:7). Circumcision was to be the external sign for those who accepted the covenant and for the individual's belonging to the People of God.

The covenant was ratified around an altar on which young bulls were sacrificed. Moses splashed half of the blood, drawn from the bulls, upon the altar (representing God) and half upon the people, saying, "This is the blood of the Covenant that Yahweh has made with you" (Ex. 24:8). This action signified the Israelites' commitment of themselves to God and their close union with him. The meal which followed signified and created a fellowship among them. In order that the people would never forget how God saved them and how much he loved them, he commanded them to celebrate a Passover ritual every year. In this celebration, they would relive the Passover and renew the covenant in their lives.

PEOPLE OF GOD

Since God rescued the Israelites from Egyptian slavery, they belonged to him and he made them his own people. They were so very much his that they were called "the sons of God." God would consider them a kingdom of priests, a consecrated nation and, like he, they would be considered "holy." They were the "anointed" of God. Israel was called the virgin bride of Yahweh, and when Israel failed to worship Yahweh, she was considered to be guilty of unfaithfulness. All these titles of Israel indicated her intimate relationship with God.

16

It is important to realize that God was concerned with forming a community. The individual was loved by God and was called to salvation, but he was called as a member of a community. In some mysterious way, Israel was one person in whom many individuals were found. God was concerned about the individual, but he was also concerned that the individuals *as a community* would obey, worship, love, and serve him. This is the reason the covenant was made not between God and individuals, but between God and a community.

PROMISED LAND

OLD COVENANT

God gave the Israelites manna and quail on their way to the Promised Land

NEW COVENANT

Jesus gives us his own body and blood as food on our way to heaven

---

The Israelites wandered through the desert for forty years before they finally came to Canaan (present day Israel), the land promised them by God. However, none of the adults who began the journey arrived at the Promised Land. After forty years in the desert, some died of hardships and others of old age. Since the people

17

were very unfaithful to God during their journey through the desert, God was preparing a new generation to enter the Promised Land. God promised them a country of their own, but it was theirs not simply for their walking into it. They achieved it by many hardships, struggles, and by fighting against the warring peoples on the way to Canaan. Throughout the journey God provided them with manna, quail, and water. They arrived in Canaan around 1200 B.C., but it took them about one hundred and fifty years before they finally overcame all the resistance of the Canaanite people.

DEEPER MEANING OF THE EXODUS-PASSOVER

Israel's exodus from Egypt was to influence and shape the rest of her existence. The importance of the Exodus cannot be exaggerated. Without the Exodus there would not be an Israelite people. While in Egypt, they were a motley group of people, enslaved, without unity, purpose, or hope. Moses came into their lives, freed them, united them, gave them a sense of purpose. He then guided them safely through the wilderness of the desert, and led them to victory over enemies along the way to the Promised Land. He gave them an identity, helped to form them into a people and to bring about the birth of the nation of Israel.

Later, the prophets reminded the Israelites that God freed them not only from political slavery but also from spiritual slavery: from sin, Egyptian idolatry, and paganism. God freed them not because of any merits of their own, but because he chose to do so. Through Moses he led them out of Egypt to the kingdom he planned for them. Through Moses he gave them the commandments and other laws to form them into a nation belonging to God. He freed them from slavery so that they would belong to him. He freed them from idolatry so that they would worship him, the true God. During their forty-year journey to the Promised Land, God cared for them, fed them, chastised them, transformed them; finally, he brought them into Jerusalem, where he dwelt in their midst in the tabernacle above the Ark of the Covenant.

No wonder the Israelites could never forget the Exodus. Every year the Israelites relived this experience at their Passover celebration which took place on the anniversary of the Exodus.

For the Israelites the Passover meal and celebration was a commemoration, a memorial service of the great Exodus event in their history. This Passover celebration, however, was not a reference merely to the past — what God had done; but also to the present — what God wants to do now; and to the future — what God will do. It meant not only celebrating what God had done in the past: it also meant bringing the Exodus to the present, in the sense of re-living, re-experiencing, re-newing it, making it happen all over again in their own lives. For this reason the Israelites, in their annual commemoration service, held to the same meal and celebration of the first Passover service. By taking part in this annual commemoration, every Jew of every generation identified himself with the community God rescued from Egypt and with which he made the covenant. By this participation, he was considered a member of God's Chosen People. Without taking part in this paschal celebration, he would not be inserting himself into the paschal mystery, and thereby would not be worthy to share in the blessings of the covenant. It amounted to the realization of the fact that God saved and chose as his people not only the Israelites of 1270 B.C., but all the Jews of every generation.

This annual celebration referred also to the future because their salvation would be completed only in the future. This celebration made them look forward to another Passover, to their final, completed salvation.

UNFAITHFULNESS OF ISRAEL —PROMISE OF A NEW COVENANT

Even though Israel was God's Chosen People and God guided Israel, her history and life were not easy. In time, especially under King Solomon, Israel reached great material prosperity. This prosperity, as often happens with individuals and nations, led to the neglect of God, even to the point of idolatry. To bring the people back to him, God sent them great spiritual men called prophets, who were the spokesmen for God. These prophets (750-587 B.C.) spoke against the people's religious hypocrisy, formalism, and mere external observances of the laws; against the lack of social justice and neighborly love; against the presumption of being saved

20

simply because they were Israelites. They condemned and threatened Israel with punishment for her infidelity to the covenant, but they preached hope when she was punished by wars, oppression, and captivity. So often was Israel unfaithful to God! So often was she punished! So often did she come back to God! And so often did God receive Israel back! God's love is so great!

Such unfaithfulness however, could not go on forever, and since Israel was not faithful to her part of the covenant, God would make a new covenant with mankind. Thus, the prophets announced and promised a better and a new covenant, a new king, and a more glorious kingdom of Israel.

Before treating the New Covenant, it is important to consider two other items about Israel, namely, her mission and what kept the people so closely bound together.

MISSION OF ISRAEL

Israel's mission was twofold, namely, to be a witness and to be a mediator. In ancient times the people had very many deities, and there was much idolatry. God, however, had separated the Israelite community from the world, consecrated it to his service, and wanted Israel to worship the one true God. Thus, Israel would be a witness to the uniqueness of God, witnessing to all people that there is only one God and him alone must everyone worship.

In God's plan, Israel was to be the chosen people through whom he would shower his blessings not only upon the Israelite community, but also upon all mankind: not only upon the Jews, but also upon the Gentiles. Through Israel God would renew with all mankind his communication and relationship ruptured by sin. Since Israel was a "priestly nation" she would be a mediator to others.

Israel was to be a religious and a worldly community: religious, because she was separated from the world and consecrated to the service of God; worldly, because through her holiness, she was to bring God to the world and the world to God.

UNITY OF ISRAEL

In studying the trying history and life of the Israelites and the continual persecution of the Jewish people even to the present day, one must be amazed at how closely-knit the people have remained. They have a wonderful spirit of unity and solidarity. Some of the factors which have bound them so much into a community are: pride in their calling, the law of Moses, and the liturgy.

The Israelites had every reason for being proud of their calling because they knew that God had chosen them personally as his people and consecrated them for his special purposes. They remained closely-knit because they were aware that God was concerned with them *as a community*, that he would work out his plan through them *as a community*.

The Mosaic laws united the people. These laws permeated their whole life and their institutions, and thereby helped them to be conscious of their unity and divine election.

Liturgy, above all, united them into a closely-knit community, because only liturgy can effect a true, deep-lasting unity. During the liturgical celebrations, they were reminded of their divine election, oneness, and purpose. The liturgy joined the people to God, and God himself would help keep them united.

TYPOLOGY OF THE EXODUS-PASSOVER

OLD TESTAMENT	NEW TESTAMENT
Moses	Jesus, the New Moses
Moses, the Liberator of the Israelites	Jesus, the Liberator of the Christians
from the bondage of the Egyptians	from the bondage of the devil and sin
unblemished lamb	unblemished Lamb of God, Jesus
blood of lamb on the doorposts	blood of Jesus on the wood of the cross
three days of darkness before Israelites were freed	three days in tomb before Jesus resurrected
crossing of Red Sea; circumcision	Baptism
cloud by day; fire by night	Jesus, Holy Spirit
manna	Holy Communion
Mosaic law	Law of love
Old Covenant	New Covenant
Passover-meal	Last Supper, Eucharist
Promised Land, Jerusalem	Heavenly Jerusalem

Chapter Two

THE NEW COVENANT

To have a deeper understanding of what we possess in the New Covenant, we must have some understanding of the Old Covenant, at least a general picture as presented in the preceding chapter. Then we shall see how God's love for us has been foreshadowed from the beginning of time. By seeing the parallel between the Old and the New Covenant, our love for God shall increase.

PARALLEL BETWEEN THE OLD AND NEW COVENANT

Christ is the new Moses who completed what the first Moses could not do. He freed us from the bondage of sin, from the power of the devil and the other fallen

25

angels. He is the Lamb of God by whose death we have been saved, and by whose flesh and blood we are nourished on our journey to the Promised Land, heaven. He is the manna, the Living Bread from heaven. He is the Temple in which dwells the fullness of divinity. The New Law of love which he gave us completed the Old Law given on Mt. Sinai. He enacted a new and an eternal covenant between God and us, completing the Mt. Sinai covenant.

OLD COVENANT

The Israelites received the law from God through Moses

NEW COVENANT

We received the law of love from God through Jesus

Christ formed us into the People of God of the New Covenant. We, the Church, are the New Israel marching through history to our Promised Land, heaven. Israel of old made her way to the Promised Land under Moses, Aaron, and Joshua; we are guided to the heavenly Jerusalem by the apostles and their successors.

Let us now consider how Christ accomplished this because, through him, with him, and in him was fulfilled the promise God made to Abraham about two thousand years before, namely, that in him all the nations of the earth will be blessed.

CHRIST IS OUR PASSOVER

As a slaughtered lamb played the main part in Israel's Passover and in her being delivered from bondage, so the slaughtered Lamb of God, Jesus, played the main part in our Passover, and in our being delivered from the bondage of sin and death. Christ is our passover (I Cor 5:7). He had undergone a "passover" for our sake. The manner of his passover was as follows: by taking upon himself our human nature, and by living our life and being obedient to the Father in all things, he "passed-over" from weakness to strength, from suffering to glory, from death to life, from earth to heaven. Through his "passover," light was victorious over darkness, life conquered death, humanity "passed-over" from slavery and death to freedom and life.

Christ became our paschal lamb through whom we have been saved. He was killed, his blood was shed, his legs were not broken, his flesh was to be eaten. We have been able to "pass-over" to the Father because, through Baptism, we share in Christ's paschal-mystery (death-resurrection-ascension).

THE LAST SUPPER

"It was before the festival of the Passover, and Jesus knew that the hour had come for him to pass from this world to the Father. He had always loved those who were his in the world, but now he showed how perfect his love was" (Jn. 13:1). And so, taking the bread and wine of the Passover meal, he said to his disciples: "I have longed to eat this passover with you before I suffer" (Lk. 22:15). There is so much similarity between the Jewish Passover meal and the Last Supper, the Eucharist (the new Passover meal): recounting the events of God's love for his people, the lamb (Christ is the Lamb), shedding of its blood (his blood), eating of its flesh (his flesh), drinking of the wine (his blood), giving thanks for God's goodness (Eucharist means thanksgiving).

OLD COVENANT

**The Israelites celebrated the Passover
in memory of God's love for them**

NEW COVENANT

**We celebrate the new passover, the Eucharist,
in memory of God's love for us in Christ**

At the Passover celebration, the father recounted the events and meaning behind the annual celebration of the Passover. The joyful singing of those present signified that what they were celebrating took place not only for the Jews of the past, but that they were and are a part of it. During the Eucharist, the prayers, readings, and the homily recount to us the events and meaning of Calvary and the Resurrection. Our joyful singing and participation in the Eucharist remind us that we also share in, and are incorporated into Christ's sacrifice and "passover." For the Jews, to participate in and to eat of the Passover

28

meal was to share in that reality. For us, to participate in the Mass and to receive Holy Communion is to share in this reality. Thus, we see the reason for taking part in the Mass and for receiving Holy Communion. Jesus said: "I tell you most solemnly, if you do not eat the flesh of the Son of Man and drink his blood, you will not have life in you" (Jn. 6:53).

God wanted the Israelites to celebrate the Passover so that they would never forget what he had done for them. Christ wants us to celebrate the Eucharist, so that we would never forget what Christ has done for us: "Do this as a memorial of me" (1 Cor. 11:25).

At the Last Supper Jesus said: "From now on, I tell you, I shall not drink wine until the day I drink the new wine with you in the kingdom of my Father" (Mt. 26:29). The Passover meal made the Israelites look to a future salvation; the Eucharist makes us look to the future when our salvation will be completed.

THE CHRISTIAN'S PASSOVER

By assuming our human nature, Christ identified himself with us, so that his passover and victory became ours. Since he assumed our human nature, we were taken up into Christ, so that we were present and included in his life, suffering, death, resurrection, and ascension – in his passover. "When we were baptized in Christ Jesus we were baptized in his death; in other words, when we were baptized we went into the tomb with him and joined him in death, so that as Christ was raised from the dead by the Father's glory, we too might live a new life" (Rom. 6:3-4). Thus, we already "passed-over" through, with, and in Christ, our Head.

This victory in Christ, however, is not ours automatically. As the Israelites had to be faithful to their covenant with God, so we must be faithful to our baptismal covenant.

At Baptism we have been "Christed," that is, we have received the life of Christ, we have "put on Christ," we have been "grafted onto Christ." Thus, we must live a Christ-like life. As Christ went through death to his resurrection, we must do likewise. We must "die" to our weak and sinful self, and "rise" to the life of the Spirit within us. And since we experience so much the effects of original sin, our life must be a continuous "passover." This means a continuous struggle against sin and temptation, against our weak, human nature; as we have so often heard, "putting off the old self and putting on the new." It is a "passing-over" from self to God.

Since Baptism identified us with Christ, our whole life must be spent in becoming more and more like him. To achieve this, we must come in contact with Christ in the Mass and the other sacraments. By receiving him, especially in Holy Communion, he will help us in our continuous "passovers," and thereby help us to become more and more like him. To become like Christ is not easy, but neither was the passover easy for the Israelites, nor for Christ. The Israelites had to pass through the desert to the Promised Land, Jerusalem; we have to pass through the desert of our life to the Promised Land, the heavenly Jerusalem.

THE NEW COVENANT

Since the Israelites were unfaithful to the Mt. Sinai covenant, God initiated a new and better covenant. This was the covenant established by Christ at the Last Supper and sealed with the shedding of his own blood (Lk. 22:20). This new covenant solemnized a deeper relationship between God and us: whereas the old covenant promised that *God would be with the Israelites*, the new covenant promised more, namely, that *besides being with us, God would give us a share in his own life*. Furthermore, this would be an everlasting covenant, as is evident from the words of Christ which are repeated at the consecration in every Mass: "This is the cup of my blood, the blood of the new and everlasting covenant."

This covenant formed a new People of God, the Church. As the Israelites belonged to the People of God through circumcision, so we belong to the People of God through baptism. As the Israelites shared in the benefits of the old covenant by participating in the Passover celebration, so we share in the benefits of the new covenant by participating in the new Passover celebration, the Eucharist.

The covenant was the very center of the lives of the Jewish people, the basis of their faith, and the basis of their very existence as a People of God. God, however, made this covenant not only with those who were at Mt. Sinai, but with all future generations. It was through the celebration of the Passover feast that each generation of Jews would enter the covenant with God. By this celebration, the events of the Passover and the covenant were made present, both in remembrance and in effect, to each generation. God did not need to renew the covenant, but every Jew of the future would have to pledge his acceptance of the covenant which God made with his forefathers. By celebrating the Passover, he said in effect: "I will do all that the Lord had said." By celebrating the Passover, he acknowledged his pact with God: "You are my God and I will be ever faithful to you."

OLD COVENANT

The old covenant was ratified with the blood of animals

NEW COVENANT

The new covenant was ratified with the blood of Jesus

Every year Christ celebrated this paschal rite. However, when he celebrated the Passover for the last time on Holy Thursday, he gave the command: "Do this *in memory of me*"; in other words, "celebrate the Passover no longer in memory of what God did for you in the past, but *in memory of what I am doing for you today and will do for you tomorrow on Calvary*." Thus, the former paschal supper became the new paschal supper, the memorial and renewal of the new covenant. The Eucharist makes present the new Passover, our deliverance from the slavery of sin and death, through the sacrifice and blood of the Lamb of God.

The new covenant, perpetuated and made present in the Eucharist, is for us the very center of our lives, the basis of our faith, and the basis of our very existence as a People of God. We become sharers in the covenant when, in Baptism, we are made one with Christ. In every Eucharist we can publicly proclaim our acceptance of the covenant. In every Eucharist we can renew our personal ratification of the covenant and seal it with the sacrifices of our daily life. In every Eucharist we can tell Christ that we want him as our Lord and Savior and that we will be faithful to him.

After the death of Jesus "the curtain of the sanctuary was torn in two from top to bottom" (Mk. 15:38). The temple of Jerusalem was the symbol of God's presence among his people. The tearing of the curtain symbolized the departure of God from the temple. The Old Testament sacrifices came to an end; the new sacrifice is the sacrifice of Calvary, renewed and re-presented in an unbloody manner in the Eucharist. The Old Testament sanctuary came to an end; the new temple of God's presence on earth is his Body, the Church. The Old Covenant gave way to the New Covenant.

THE NEW PEOPLE OF GOD

Since Christ rescued us from the slavery of sin and death, we belong to him, and he has made us his own people. St. Peter tells us: "You are a chosen race, a royal priesthood, a consecrated nation, a people set apart to sing the praises of God who called you out of the darkness into his wonderful light. Once you were not a people at all and now you are the People of God" (1 Pt. 2:9-10).

33

We are a more sublime reality than that of the People of God of the Old Testament. In the Old Testament, only the Jews belonged to the People of God, in the New Testament, Jews and Gentiles; in the Old Testament, membership depended upon circumcision, in the New Testament, on Baptism; in the Old Testament, salvation "came from the Jews," in the New Testament, "from the Church."

Through Christ, God formed us into a community. This concept of a corporate person, initiated by God with the Israelites, is fulfilled in us, the Body of Christ, the Church. The Church grows when people are incorporated into Christ through Baptism, and when they live with the life of the risen Lord. Since this includes everyone baptized in Christ, the new People of God includes all those on earth, in heaven, and in purgatory.

Because of this corporate personality, we have the doctrine of the Communion of Saints, whereby our lives have an influence upon each other, on earth, in heaven, and in purgatory. We are able to help each other by our prayers, sacrifices, by our good life. We have an influence and are dependent upon each other, for better or for worse. Hence, by our virtuous or mediocre living, we build up or weaken the Body of Christ. What an awesome truth! What a great responsibility for us to live a truly Christian life!

God does not want to sanctify us and save us merely as individuals. He formed us into a community, and we are sanctified and saved also as members of this community, the Church. The Church is one person in whom many individuals are found. Though God is *concerned about the individual, he is also concerned that the individuals as a community* would obey, worship, love, and serve him.

It can be said more of us than of Israel that we are "the sons of God" (through Christ we have become the sons and daughters of the Father); a kingdom of priests (sharing in Christ's priesthood); a consecrated nation (washed in Christ's precious blood); "anointed of God" (anointed at Baptism); "holy" (we share in the divine life); the virgin bride of Christ (the Church is the Bride of Christ). Hence, when we fail to worship God and fail to fulfill his will, we are guilty of unfaithfulness.

THE PROMISED LAND

God promised us not an earthly Jerusalem, as he had promised the Israelites, but a heavenly Jerusalem. However, heaven will be ours only if we are faithful to God, and if we are victorious in our struggle against ourselves and against the powers of the world of darkness. Our life must be a continuous "passover." We must learn from the Israelites who never entered the Promised Land, namely, that heaven will not be ours simply because we are the People of God.

Israel of old made her way through the desert to the Promised Land under the divinely appointed leaders – Moses, Aaron, and Joshua; we are guided by the divinely appointed leaders in the person of Peter and his successors. And as God provided for the Israelites during their march through the desert by providing them with manna, quail, and water, so he provides for us by giving us the Church and the sacraments, to refresh, strengthen, and encourage us on our march through the desert of life, on our way to heaven.

OUR UNFAITHFULNESS – NEW COVENANT SUFFICIENT

Throughout the two thousand years of Christian history, there has been much unfaithfulness on our part. The evils the prophets of old spoke against are still with us. Looking into our own lives and upon the life of the Church, we still see religious hypocrisy (e.g., calling ourselves Christians, but not living as Christians); formalism (e.g., praying with our lips but not with our heart); legalism (e.g., going to church on Sundays because we have to). We still see a great lack of social justice and neighborly love (poverty, prejudice, greed, and selfishness).

The new covenant of Christ, however, is sufficient. It is all we need. His covenant is the "blood of the new and everlasting covenant." We need but to learn the meaning of Christianity – Passover, Covenant, Baptism, Eucharist.

MISSION OF THE CHURCH

As for Israel of old so for the Church her mission is twofold, namely, to be a witness and to be a mediator. Through Christ we have received the revelation of the true God. We are to give witness of this to the world. But are we a witness of this great reality which we possess? Does the world see that we are different from it? The Church must be holy in order to witness to the holiness it possesses through Christ. The world has many gods today: money, power, sex, sports, athletes, models, musical groups, television, and so forth. We must be a witness, a "sign" to the world of the true God, that he is first, above everything else. The world is crying and dying for community and for meaningful social living. We must witness to the world that community is possible, and possible only through Christ, in union with the Father and the Holy Spirit.

In the Old Testament salvation "came from the Jews," whereas in the New Testament salvation "comes from the Church." Hence, the Church is to be a mediator to the world. The Church must be the light of the world and the salt of the earth. The Church must christianize and transform the world, bringing Christ's risen life into all its spheres. We can do this by real, mature, Christian living, especially by selfless loving. Christ said that by loving each other people will know that we are his disciples. Many early pagans converted to Christianity when they saw how the Christians loved each other. It is through Christian love that we will bring God's love and life to the world.

The Church is to be a religious and worldly community; religious, because she possesses the holiness of God, is the Body of Christ, is separated from the world and is consecrated to the service of God; worldly, because through her holiness she is to bring God to the world and the world to God.

UNITY OF THE CHURCH

The Jewish people had and still have a wonderful spirit of unity and solidarity. Our unity and solidarity, however, is stronger and more wonderful. Through Baptism we have been incorporated into the Body of Christ: "There is one Body, one Spirit, just as you were all called into one and the same hope . . . There is one Lord, one faith, one baptism, and one God who is Father of all, over all, through all, and within all" (Eph. 4:4-5).

OLD COVENANT

The Jews (Israelites) are still waiting for the promised redeemer

NEW COVENANT

We are awaiting the Second Coming of Jesus

The children of Israel were closely-knit because of their pride in their calling, the law of Moses, and their liturgy. We should be even more closely-knit than the Israelites, and for similar reasons. We should be proud of being called into the Body of Christ, of being a community through which Christ brings salvation to the world. We must try to remember that we, *as a community*, are a chosen *people* of God, a consecrated *nation*, a priestly *nation*. Through their annual Passover celebration, the Israelites were reminded of their great calling; in our eucharistic celebration we learn and are reminded of our great calling.

Christ has given us the law of love; therefore, we are to love each other as he loves us. He has given us the law of love to unite us more closely into a community. Since we are members of each other, all belonging to the Body of Christ, is it not scandalous that we have so little love for each other?

Our liturgy, above all, should help to form us into a community. In the Eucharist we come into contact with Christ to strengthen our union with him and with each other. Since only Christ can unite us, and since we are a priestly nation, community worship is vital for us in order to experience and strengthen our unity and solidarity. It is true that on Sunday we may appear like a community, but how is it in reality? Do we celebrate the Eucharist as a community? Or, do we pray as so many individuals? Are we like one family? Or, are we like strangers to each other, even to those with whom we worship Sunday after Sunday?

THE EUCHARISTIC MIRACLE
"The Host changed into Flesh, the Wine into Blood"
LANCIANO

see p. 66

Chapter Three

THE MASS

Active and intelligent participation in the eucharistic liturgy must be both interior and exterior. For such participation we must have some understanding of: 1) salvation history; 2) the Body of Christ; 3) the terms: People of God, Covenant, Passover; 4) Christ as our mediator with the Father; 5) sharing in Christ's priesthood; 6) the importance of corporate worship; 7) the Eucharist as the best prayer, the best form of worship.

The first two chapters have intended to present this fundamental and most important understanding. However, this chapter and the following one, taken by themselves, will nonetheless, give one much understanding of the Eucharist.

MASS: BANQUET AND SACRIFICE

The Mass has the character of a banquet through which the Lord's Supper and his sacrifice of the cross are perpetuated and made present in our midst. It is a banquet in the sense that we come together as one family to express our thanks and praise for all of God's goodness and his love for us; to listen and to respond to him as he teaches and nourishes us at the table of the word and gives us his body and blood at the table of the Eucharist; to share in his life and the life of each other; to be strengthened and encouraged to work for the extension of God's kingdom in the world.

The Mass is a prayer not to Jesus

but a prayer of Jesus and his Church to the Father

It is a sacrifice because of its relationship with the sacrifice of the cross, and because it is an offering of that same sacrifice. "At the Last Supper our Savior instituted the eucharistic sacrifice of his body and blood to perpetuate the sacrifice of the cross throughout the centuries until he comes again. He entrusted it to his bride, the Church, as a memorial of his death and resurrection" (*GI*, 2). As the eternally glorified victim, Christ continues to offer himself, rendering praise and thanksgiving to the Father, and interceding for all mankind.

RELATIONSHIP BETWEEN CALVARY AND THE MASS

It is *not a new* sacrifice *nor another* sacrifice. Calvary and the Mass are one and the same sacrifice offered under two different forms: formerly, in a bloody manner; now, in an unbloody manner. It may help us to understand this if we keep in mind that in the Mass we continue to do what Christ did at the Last Supper, when he offered himself in anticipation of his sacrifice on Good Friday. The Mass is both the "Lord's Supper" and the "sacrifice of his body and blood." (*GI*, 2). It adds nothing to Christ's sacrifice in the sense that something was lacking on Calvary. We do not add to it, as if his sacrifice on Calvary were not infinite and needed our help!

Calvary and the Mass has infinite value —

But the fruits of the Mass depend

upon how I participate in it

What then is new in the Mass? First, the Mass makes Christ's sacrifice present to us. It is a memorial of Calvary, not in the sense of merely recalling what happened nearly two thousand years ago, but in the sense of perpetuating and making present the sacrifice of the cross upon our altars. Second, on Calvary we have only the death of Christ, whereas in the Mass we celebrate the paschal mystery of Christ – his death and resurrection. Third, we were redeemed on Calvary, whereas in the Mass we come in contact with our Savior, and through this contact we receive the fruits of his sacrifice. It possesses all the merits of Christ's sacrifice, and these are now applied to the actual and present needs of the world. Fourth, the sacrifice of Calvary was offered solely by Christ, whereas the Mass is offered by Christ and his Church; and, whereas the sacrifice of Calvary and the Mass is infinite in value, the fruits of the Mass depend upon the faith and dispositions with which the Church offers the eucharistic sacrifice.

ENDS OF THE MASS

When our first parents sinned by disobedience, we and all creation were turned away from God. Neither we nor creation could return to God without divine assistance. We could not render proper worship to God.

I want to offer my P A R T in the Mass

I want to be a P A R T in the Mass

There was a breakdown not only between God and us and creation, but also within ourselves, with others, and with creation. We and creation needed redemption. The purpose of Calvary was to bring about the needed reconciliation. The Mass, a perpetuation of Calvary, has the same purpose. "It is at once a sacrifice of praise and of thanksgiving, a sacrifice that reconciles us to the Father and makes amends to him for the sins of the world" (*GI*, 2).

44

For our purpose here, it will be good to know the four ends of the Mass mentioned by St. Thomas of Aquinas, namely, adoration, thanksgiving, reparation, and petition. It may be difficult, while celebrating the Eucharist, to remember these ends, but we can easily remember them by a simple method. By taking the first letter of each word, we can form the word P A R T. As we prepare ourselves to go to church, we can keep before ourselves the thought, "I am going to church because I want to *offer my* P A R T *in the Mass*; I want to offer my petition, adoration, reparation, and thanksgiving." Furthermore, since we are to offer ourselves in the Mass, we can keep before ourselves the thought, "I am going to Mass because I want to *be a* P A R T *of the Mass*; I want to offer *myself* in union with Christ, as a victim and mediator for all the petitions, adoration, reparation, and thanksgiving of Christ and the world."

MASS: THE CHURCH'S SACRIFICE AND PASSOVER

Christ continues to offer his sacrifice through his Church in the Mass. His work of redemption was not something only of the past, done once and for all. By offering himself and us to the Father, Christ continues his work of redemption, reconciliation, and sanctification.

His sacrifice is ours, and we are able to offer the eucharistic sacrifice because of our Baptism. In Baptism we received the life of Christ, so that we are truly "other Christs." Hence, he gives us a share in his life and work. Jesus, the Priest, lets us share in his priesthood, and thus we must offer him and ourselves as worship of the

Father. Jesus, the Victim, lets us share in his victimhood, and thus we must offer ourselves as victims, in union with the Victim Christ. Jesus, the Mediator, lets us share in his mediatorship, and thus we must offer ourselves as mediators for the salvation of the world.

Through Baptism we have become a priestly people, a worshiping community whose duty and privilege it is to offer sacrifice to the heavenly Father. "Jesus Christ . . . washed away our sins with his blood, and made us a line of kings, priests to serve his God and Father . . ."

Baptism makes me priest — victim — mediator

(Rv. 1:5). We are a "holy priesthood that offers the spiritual sacrifices which Jesus Christ has made acceptable to God . . . a chosen race, a royal priesthood, a consecrated nation, a people set apart to sing the praises of God . . ." (1 Pt. 2:5, 9). It is our duty and privilege to offer the eucharistic sacrifice.

The Mass is the Church's Passover because in it we offer to the Father his Son, our Paschal Lamb, who continues his redemptive work in us. However, we must cooperate in this redemptive work: we must continue in our lives the "passover," the return to the Father inaugurated by Christ. We must freely and consciously unite ourselves and our whole life to Christ's sacrifice. Thus, with him we will "pass-over" from this world and from our "self" to the Father in heaven. By uniting our

46

daily living with Christ in the Eucharist, we will live and die and resurrect with him and come to be united with the heavenly Father.

Christ, however, is concerned not only with individual redemption, but also with social redemption. All of society must be redeemed. Through the Eucharist we

---

I don't get anything out of the Mass! —

But do you put anything into the Mass?

---

can acquire the vision and grace of Christ to help redeem society according to Christian principles. By acquiring the dispositions of Christ – love, obedience, and self-sacrifice – we will become involved in the work of helping to redeem society.

PARTS OF THE MASS

The Mass comprises two distinct, though related parts, namely, Liturgy of the Word and Liturgy of the Eucharist. The one centers around the Bible, and other, around the bread and wine. However, both form one single act of worship. They are not independent of each other. What is proclaimed in the Liturgy of the Word is celebrated in the Liturgy of the Eucharist. Christ is present in both parts; first in his word, then in his eucharistic action.

Christ said that man does not live by bread alone, but by every word that issues from the mouth of God. This word is our food before the eucharistic bread: we receive Christ in the sacred readings before receiving him in Holy Communion.

St. Augustine very aptly shows the relationship between the word of God and Holy Communion. He asks his congregation: "What seems greater to you: the word of God or the body of Christ?" And he answers: "If you want to say the truth, you must always say that the word of God is not less than the body of Christ." He adds: "Whoever hears the word of God negligently is not less culpable than he who carelessly allows the body of Christ to fall on the ground."

Which seems greater: the word of God or the body of Christ?

The first part of the Mass is the Liturgy of the Word. The purpose of the readings and the homily is to proclaim the word of God, which has power to change our lives. We are not simply to listen, but to respond to what is being proclaimed. The living word is no less powerful today than in the past, for God is the same yesterday, today, and forever. Hence, no other reading, no matter how beautiful it may be or how eloquently delivered, can accomplish such a change in us as can the word of God. The purpose of the Liturgy of the Word is not information, but transformation; not merely to tell what God has done in the past, but what he continues to do today; not merely to instruct, but to lead to worship.

The Liturgy of the Word is a celebration of what God has done for us, so that we can respond to that word by sacrifice in the second part of the Mass. Worship is not something we do for God; rather it is our response to what he has done for us. But to respond properly we must know what God has done for us, and we must recall it to mind frequently. This is one of the functions of the Liturgy of the Word. By arousing our faith, love, and devotion, we are able to participate more fervently in the liturgical celebration. Thus, the Liturgy of the Word and the Liturgy of the Eucharist complement and complete each other.

The second part of the Mass, Liturgy of the Eucharist, begins with the preparation of the gifts and ends before the concluding rite. It is the heart of the entire liturgical celebration. The word "eucharist" means "thanksgiving." Hence, in this second part, we thank God for the whole work of reconciliation and salvation.

PREPARATION OF THE GIFTS (Offertory)

In order that we may receive the graces of redemption, there must be in ourselves a death to sin which was brought about on the cross. We begin this death to sin by offering ourselves in union with Christ. We can offer ourselves, for example, in the following words: "Heavenly Father, in union with your beloved Son, Jesus Christ, I offer you my intellect, my will, my body, soul, and spirit; my talents, my work, my aspirations, my struggles, crosses, sorrows, joys, sacrifices, prayers, everything, especially _____." St. Paul said:

"Whatever you eat, whatever you drink, whatever you do at all, do it for the glory of God" (1 Cor. 10:31). Hence, our whole life can and should be a continuous offering which glorifies God, ever increases our union with him, and draws blessings upon ourselves and the world. Since we do not have time to formulate our offering during the liturgy, we should get into the habit of doing so even before we come to church.

The offering of ourselves is made symbolically by the presentation of the bread and wine from the congregation. Archbishop Sheen shows the depth of meaning of this action in the following words: "Two of the substances which have most widely nourished man are bread and wine. Bread has been called the marrow of the earth; wine, its very blood. In giving what has traditionally made our flesh and blood, we are equivalently offering all mankind on the paten . . .

"Before the bread could be placed on the paten and wine poured into the chalice, how many elements of the economic, financial and technical world had to be brought into play! The wheat needed farmers, fields, sacks, trucks, mills, commerce, finance, buying and selling. The grapes required vineyards, bottles, wine-presses, time, space, chemistry, a thousand years of accumulated skills.

". . . therefore, we gather up the whole world into the narrow compass of a plate and a cup. Every drop of sweat, every day of labor, the decisions of the economist, the financier, the draughtsman and the engineer, every exertion and invention that went into the preparation of

50

the elements of the Offertory are symbolically re-deemed, justified and sanctified by our act. We bring not only redeemed man, but . . . (all) creation to the steps of Calvary and the threshold of Redemption" (*The Priest is Not His Own*, pp. 34-35).

The presentation of the gifts and the accompanying prayers of the priest, however, is not the *offering* of the Mass. It is but the initial stage preparing the material for the sacrifice, and the symbolic expression of uniting ourselves with the sacrifice of Christ. The offering (sacrifice) takes place in the Eucharistic Prayer, at the consecration, when Christ becomes present on our altars as Victim and Priest.

In the Mass we offer not only Jesus,

but ourselves, all humanity, and all creation

(The Eucharist is the sacrifice of the Church alone, insofar as only those who believe may share in it. Thus, the Church alone in her living members is united to Christ in his eucharistic sacrifice. On the other hand, however, the Eucharist is the sacrifice of the whole human race, insofar as Christ died for all and wants all to be saved and to receive the graces of his death and resurrection. Hence, since Christ includes all mankind and all creation in his sacrifice, we should not simply offer ourselves, but all humanity and all creation.)

After the gifts have been prepared the priest says: "Pray, brethren, that our sacrifice may be acceptable to God, the almighty Father." But our response, "May the Lord accept the sacrifice at your hands for the praise and glory of his name, for our good, and the good of all his Church," cannot be meaningful unless we have really offered ourselves. And the Lord himself gives us the condition for the acceptance of our gifts: "If you are bringing your offering to the altar and there remember that your brother has something against you, leave your offering there before the altar, go and be reconciled with your brother first, and then come back and present your offering" (Mt. 5:23-24).

EUCHARISTIC PRAYER

"The eucharistic prayer, a prayer of thanksgiving and sanctification, is the center and high point of the entire celebration. In an introductory dialogue the priest invites the people to lift their hearts to God in prayer and thanks; he unites them with himself in the prayer he addresses in their name to the Father through Jesus Christ. The meaning of the prayer is that the whole congregation joins Christ in acknowledging the works of God and in offering the sacrifice" (*GI*, 54).

After the preface, the priest prays that, through the power of the Holy Spirit, our gifts of bread and wine may become the body and blood of Christ. And, as Christ is with us in his eucharistic presence, he continues his work of reconciliation: "this is my body which will be given up for you . . . this is the cup of my blood . . . it will be shed for you and for all so that sins may be forgiven."

After our acclamation of the mystery of faith –
"Christ has died, Christ is risen, Christ will come
again," – we offer to the Father "this life-giving bread,
this saving cup . . . this holy and living sacrifice." In
union with Christ and through him, we offer ourselves to
the Father, so that we could become more perfectly
united with him and with each other and that, eventually, God may be all in all. Then we pray for the Church
and its members, living and deceased. The eucharistic
prayer concludes with the doxology, to which the people
respond with a solemn *Amen*.

CONSECRATION

The Eucharistic Prayer is centered in the consecration. The consecration, changing of the bread and wine
into the body and blood of Christ, brings us many
spiritual riches. Let us consider some of them.

1) With the consecration, the paschal mystery – the
death and resurrection of Christ – is re-presented (made
present) upon our altars. Christ is present with the
infinite merits of his whole life. After our gifts of bread
and wine are changed into his body and blood, he gives
himself, the merits of his sacrifice and his whole life into
our hands, that we may offer him to the heavenly Father
for our salvation. Christ offers himself now through and
with his Church.

2) The consecration also affects our self-offering.
As Bishop Sheen explained it so meaningfully, the words
of consecration have a double signification. The primary
signification is that "This is the body of Christ; this is the

blood of Christ." The secondary signification concerns ourselves, namely, "This is *my* body; this is *my* blood." By uniting ourselves with the Victim Christ, we give to him all that we are and all that we have. We ask him to offer us in union with himself to the Father, so that, dying to self, we can give ourselves completely to him, saying, "Here is my body; here is my blood" and rise to a newness of life.

The essence of Christianity is to live out the paschal mystery of Christ in our lives; that is, as Christ died, resurrected and ascended into glory, so that we, too, would offer ourselves to God, die to sin and self, resurrect to a new life and, eventually, to live in eternal glory with him.

3) Since Christ offers not only himself but all the members of his Body, all who are in the state of grace are offered, even though they are not present at Mass. What a tremendous offering takes place in every Mass! The Holy Father, the bishops, priests, religious, saintly parents, struggling teenagers, innocent children; rich and poor; the learned and the unlearned; saints and struggling sinners; with all their love, prayers, sacrifices, sufferings . . . their whole life! Since we are offered by Christ in every Mass, we should try to lead a good and holy life in order to always be as pure and as pleasing an offering as possible.

4) Since Christ takes unto himself all our personal offerings, everything about us becomes transformed: our work becomes his work; our crosses, his crosses; our

suffering, his suffering; our joys, his joys; our pardons, his pardons; our prayer, his prayer; our love, his love; our life, his life. Our whole life can acquire a divine value, because he takes our offering and makes it his own: our life and actions become the life and actions of Christ.

---

the paschal mystery is perpetuated

"this is my body . . . this is my blood"

**Conse-
cration**   **with Christ we are offered to the Father**

our life can acquire divine and redemptive value

radiating P A R T

Furthermore, our whole life and its activities can acquire a redemptive value. Everything we do, no matter how insignificant, when offered to the Father in union with Christ, helps towards our redemption. In other words, we become "more and more redeemed" – depending upon how much and what we have offered of ourselves – "passing-over" more and more from the "old self to the new," from the natural to the supernatural, from self to God.

However, this divine and redemptive transformation is to be not only an individual blessing. The whole world must be divinized and redeemed, Hence, we all must participate and share in this transforming and redeeming work of Christ. Giving a piece of the world (wine, bread, ourselves) to be changed into the body and blood of Christ is but a symbol of the whole of reality that must be transformed. Thus, we must go into the world and continue there what took place on the altar.

5) With the consecration, the four ends of the Mass (P A R T) are realized; adoration, thanksgiving, reparation, and petition. The eucharistic sacrifice becomes like a powerful transmitting station, sending its invisible rays far and wide, with repercussions in heaven, purgatory, and on earth.

HOLY COMMUNION

"Since the eucharistic celebration is the paschal meal, in accord with his command, the body and blood of the Lord should be received as spiritual food by the faithful who are properly disposed" (*GI*, 56).

Since receiving Holy Communion is a sharing in the sacrifice and is its highest form of participation, we should not lightly refrain from receiving Holy Communion.

We have offered a gift of ourselves to the heavenly Father; in Holy Communion God gives us a gift of himself through Jesus Christ. We have offered his sacrifice for our salvation; in Holy Communion we share in that sacrifice. We have offered our love and obedience to the

Father; in Holy Communion we receive Christ in order to help us to persevere in carrying out our self-offering. In the Mass the Church offers and is being offered; in Holy Communion a greater union with Christ and with all the members of his Body is effected.

Jesus said: "I tell you most solemnly, if you do not eat the flesh of the Son of Man and drink his blood you will not have life in you" (Jn. 6:53). — "I tell you most solemnly . . ."

that is, he meant it!

Archbishop Fulton J. Sheen puts it very beautifully, when he says: "In the Offertory . . . (we are) like a lamb led to the slaughter. In the Consecration . . . (we are) the lamb slaughtered as the sacrificial victim. In the Communion . . . (we find that we have) not died at all, that . . . (we have) on the contrary really come to the abundant life which is union with Christ. . . . We find that our death was after all no more permanent in the Consecration than was the death of Calvary, for Holy Communion is a kind of Easter. We give up our time, and get his eternity; we give up our sin, and receive his grace; we give up petty loves, and receive the Flame of Love.

"In this union with Christ we are not alone, for Communion is not merely the union of the individual soul and Christ; it unites Christ to all the members of the Mystical Body and in an extended way through prayer to all humanity" (*Ibid.*, pp. 36-37).

FRUITFUL RECEPTION OF HOLY COMMUNION

Holy Communion makes Christ present, living and operative among us. He comes to us as our risen Lord and Savior to share his life with us and to help us in our "passing-over" to the Father. Since we need continuous saving in our daily life, he comes to continue his redemptive work which he accomplished while on earth: to enable us to see, to speak, to hear, to walk, to be cleansed, to be brought back to life. If we would but receive him and accept him as our Lord and Savior! Our "Amen" to the celebrant's "The body of Christ" means "It is true." We express, thereby, our faith that we come in contact with our Lord and Savior who desires to continue his redemptive work in us.

Christ works in us through Holy Communion, but this does not mean that we automatically receive more graces or automatically become better. The fruit of the sacraments depends upon our dispositions. Therefore, it is not the quantity, but the quality of our Holy Communions which is important. To receive "the more often the better" is true only insofar as we have the proper dispositions. Some of us may receive very little, if any fruit from Holy Communion because we may receive routinely and mechanically without any preparation or thanksgiving, with little faith or love, or with little understanding of the purpose of receiving Holy Communion. Simply to be free of serious sin is not sufficient to benefit fully from Holy Communion.

Christ's activity in Holy Communion is more important than ours, for it is he who transforms us into himself, and not vice-versa; but we must surrender, consciously give ourselves to him in order that he may transform us. We must receive Holy Communion not as "something" in order to receive more graces or a higher place in heaven, but rather as "Someone," "the Living Christ" who comes to transform us. We must stand before Christ as we are, and ask him to change us: to help us become better, to become holier, to become more patient, kind, loving, and considerate; to help us overcome temptations more quickly; to help us to be more concerned about others, about the poor and needy, and about the sorry plight of so many throughout the world.

There are many things in our life which we do not want to give up: jealousy, hatred, bitterness, pride, critical attitude, spitefulness, white lies, uncooperativeness, overindulgence of the senses, and many other sins and imperfections. These also hinder us from receiving Holy Communion more fruitfully. Thus, we must allow the Lord to change these things in our life.

Futhermore, we must try to live the Mass throughout the entire day and week, we must faithfully try to live out the "offering of ourselves" which we made.

However, the graces of Holy Communion are not only personal but especially communal. This is evident from the Eucharistic Prayers: "May all of us who share in the body and blood of Christ be brought together in unity by the Holy Spirit" (II). "Grant that we, who are nourished by his body and blood, may be filled with his Holy Spirit, and become one body, one spirit in Christ" (III). "Lord, . . . by your Holy Spirit, gather all who share this one bread and one cup into the one body of Christ, a living sacrifice of praise" (IV). As St. Paul says: "The bread that we break is a communion with the body of Christ. The fact that there is only one loaf means that, though there are many of us, we form a single body because we all have a share in this one loaf" (1 Cor. 10:16-17).

"THE MASS IS ENDED — GO IN PEACE!"

The Mass is never really ended because there is only one sacrifice and only one Eternal, High Priest and Victim who, without ceasing, offers himself to the Father. Even after our redemption has been completed,

---

"The Mass is ended!"

The Mass is not ended — it must continue in our daily life

---

he will still offer himself, however, no longer for reparation or petition, but only for adoration and thanksgiving.

It does not end when we are dismissed by the priest; it must continue in our daily life. We have offered ourselves to God and now we must live out that offering.

After having received the Lord's blessing, and even more so after having received him in Holy Communion, Christ comes with us, into our life and world, to help us live out our offering and to help bring him to the world and the world to him.

Christ tells us "Go! live the Mass! live out the offering of yourself!" We have offered him our eyes, therefore we must be careful at what we look, for our eyes are consecrated to God. We have offered him our ears, tongue, legs, arms, our whole body, therefore we must be careful how we use them, for they belong to God. We have offered him our soul with its faculties, therefore we must orient our soul towards the Lord. We have surrendered ourselves to the will of God, therefore we must learn how to accept life with all its demands, hardships, and

---

"Go in peace!"

I came to Mass alone, heavy and depressed

I leave the Mass with Christ, and in peace

---

joys, for the glory of God. Our whole life must be so lived and every action must be so performed that we can offer them to God.

However, we cannot be concerned solely about ourselves; we must help to bring Christ to the world and the world to Christ. We can begin to do this by trying to have a Christian influence on those around us; for example, parents in the home; teachers in the school;

61

workers in the office or factory; all of us among our classmates, friends, associates, relatives. Once we have made an influence in our immediate surroundings, we should try to reach out further . . . into our neighborhood, parish, city, state, national, and international levels. Indeed, we must get involved in the social ills of society because Christ came to save all mankind.

Christ tells us "Go in peace!" Yes, we can go in peace because Christ is coming with us to help us live our life. We can go in peace because we will no longer be alone, for Christ will be with us to help us to work; to bear our crosses, our headaches, our heartaches; to fight temptations; to live our Christian life. We can go in peace because, when we are not loved by others, he will love us; slighted by others, he will accept us; discouraged, he will encourage us; dejected, he will lift us up.

Indeed, the Mass makes a difference in our life because it becomes a life lived in union with Christ! Indeed, it makes a difference because "it is no longer I who live, but Christ who lives in me!"

WHY WE SHOULD "GO TO MASS"

There are many reasons why we should "go to Mass." It is hoped that one or another of the following reasons will motivate us to a better participation in the eucharistic celebration.

1) Since the work of our salvation is commemorated and continued in the Mass, gratitude demands that we take part in the eucharistic liturgy.

2) Christ saved us, but he did not intend to save us without our cooperation. The purpose of the Eucharist is not only to renew Christ's sacrifice, but also to join the sacrifice of ourselves to his, in order to indicate our desire and cooperation to be saved.

3) If we believe that Christ redeemed us, we should desire to publicly profess this belief by taking an active part in the Mass which continues his redemptive work.

4) Since Christ distributes his redemptive graces most abundantly in the Mass, it is necessary that we should come into vital contact with him in the Mass, in order to receive all the graces he desires to impart to us.

I was not on Calvary to thank Jesus for dying for me —

but I can thank him during Mass

---

5) At Baptism we have received a share in the divine life, but we need Jesus in Holy Communion in order to maintain and develop this life; for, as he said: "I tell you most solemnly, if you do not eat the flesh of the Son of Man and drink his blood, you will not have life in you" (Jn. 6:53).

6) Through Baptism we share in the priesthood of Christ. The function of the priesthood is to worship and offer sacrifice. Hence, it is our vocation, privilege, and duty to offer the eucharistic sacrifice.

7) Only perfect worship is worthy of the heavenly Father, and only the Mass is perfect worship. Not even the greatest amount of prayers, recited with the greatest devotion, can come close to the value of even one Mass.

8) Finally, some may say, "Why should I go to church? I can pray anywhere, and I can pray by myself." True, we can pray anywhere and by ourselves, but we should also worship with others because through Baptism we have become members of the Christian community. We should go to church in order to receive Holy Communion which is necessary for our spiritual life. We should go to church because, aside from a few exceptions, we do there something which we do not do anyplace else, namely, offer the best prayer, the best form of worship, the holy sacrifice of the Mass.

THOSE WHO CANNOT ATTEND MASS

In the Eucharist, Christ offers everyone who is in the state of grace, even though the person is not present in church. For this reason, we can unite ourselves with Christ in the Mass at any moment of the day. However, this does not mean that we should neglect attending church, for there is a great difference between coming into physical and spiritual contact with Christ during the Mass and coming only into spiritual contact with Christ apart from the Mass.

There are many people, however, who would like to attend church but who are unable, as for example, the sick, the oppressed, workers, and many others. These, nonetheless, are very much present at Mass, even though they are physically absent. In fact, they can be "more present" than those who are actually present. They need not be physically present in order to offer themselves in the Mass. As long as they are trying to live a life of faith, love, and surrender, they are continually present, and are being offered by Christ in every Mass. Furthermore, they can contribute even more to the eucharistic sacrifice than those actually present

---

Many cannot attend church —

but they can be present at Mass

---

because, in many instances, especially with the sick and oppressed, theirs is a perfect sacrificial offering, patterned after the love and life of Christ.

Many such individuals would very much like to receive sacramental Communion daily but cannot. However, by their acts of faith, love, and desire, such individuals can receive the Lord spiritually. This spiritual communion can produce the effects of sacramental Communion, its graces, virtues, and union with the Lord, depending upon the dispositions of the individual. After all, we ought not limit Christ's power of communing with us only through sacramental Communion. Certainly, Christ does not want to deprive such individuals from receiving him because they are unable to attend church and receive him under the form of bread and wine.

THE EUCHARISTIC MIRACLE OF LANCIANO

In the eighth century a Basilian monk in Lanciano, Italy, was tormented by involuntary doubts about the Real Presence after he had pronounced the words of consecration. One day, however, as he pronounced the words of consecration, the host changed to a flesh color, except in the center, where the host remained white; the wine changed to a blood-red color, coagulating into five small clots of varied size. The host changed into Flesh and the wine into Blood.

In 1713 the host-Flesh was enclosed in a silver monstrance, and the Blood was put in a crystal chalice, affixed to the base of the monstrance. This miracle can still be seen in the church of St. Francis in Lanciano.

Since 1574 there were four official Church investigations of the Sacred Species, but the most revealing was the one of November, 1970. A team of laboratory research men from several Italian universities was headed by Professor Edward Linoli, chief of the medical staff of research and of the board of doctors at the Arezzo General Hospital. The scientific report was published in the *L'Osservatore Romano* of April 3, 1971.

The conclusions of this investigation are as follows: 1) the Blood in the chalice is real blood and the Flesh in the monstrance is real flesh; 2) the Flesh is composed of cardiac muscle tissue; 3) the Blood and Flesh are both human; 4) the Blood and the Flesh come from the same individual; 5) the proteins in the Blood are in normal ratio as in fresh normal blood; 6) the blood chemistry is of normal human pattern.

66

Chapter Four

FORGIVENESS AND HEALING

IN THE MASS

Though the Eucharist is a communal act of worship, nonetheless, as individuals, we feel the need to be personally involved in, and to personally benefit from it. And to the extent that this need is met, to that extent will we contribute better to the worship of the community. The following explanation will help to fulfill this need.

The Mass is called the *Eucharist*, which means *thanksgiving*. Hence, we take part in it in order to thank God for all he has done for us through his Son, Jesus

Christ. We also express our praise and worship of the Father, ask his forgiveness for our sins and infidelities, and present to him our various petitions and needs.

The Eucharist is a celebration of the paschal mystery of Christ. Thus, what Christ accomplished through his death and resurrection, he continues to do in the Mass. In this chapter we shall show how he continues to save us, to forgive us our sins and to heal us. If we are conscious of the words of the liturgy, we shall see how they remind us of this continuing work of Christ in our lives.

Christ forgives us our sins in the Mass. The liturgy reminds us of our sinfulness and weakness and, at the same time, of the Lord's desire to forgive us our sins and help us with his grace. Thus it seeks to help us benefit as much as possible from the Eucharist. The saints considered themselves to be the greatest sinners. Realizing that they were not able to do anything of themselves, they threw themselves completely upon the Savior, and he helped them and raised them up to such heights of sanctity. The more we see the truth about ourselves and realize who our Savior is and the reason that he is present in the eucharistic liturgy, the more will we benefit from it.

"I confess . . ." At the very beginning we are made conscious of our sinfulness and weakness, when the priest invites us to ask the Lord's forgiveness that we may worthily offer the holy sacrifice. After we make our confession, the priest prays: "May almighty God have mercy on us, forgive us our sins, and bring us to ever-

68

lasting life." This confession is not a substitute for sacramental confession which we should not neglect. The Lord does forgive us our sins in the Mass, but in order that we may experience the Lord's forgiveness, we must be careful that our confession would not become routine, mere words. This can easily happen because we make our confession so quickly after the words of the priest inviting us to ask the Lord's forgiveness.

Our confession will be more meaningful and fruitful if we will take time to think of our sins and failures. Since we do not have sufficient time to do this during the Mass, let us make an examen of our life on our way to the church or before the beginning of the eucharistic celebration.

Furthermore, we will experience much healing in our individual lives, in our families, in our parishes if we will be conscious of the words of our confession and desire to sincerely mean these words. We confess not only to God but also "to each other." Hence, if there are in our lives any disagreements with others, any sinful relationships, any unforgiveness, any sin we do not want to give up, our "confession" cannot be sincere. Without a desire of amendment, our "confession" will be simply words and our "participation" in the Eucharist shallow. But if we want to make a sincere confession, with a firm purpose of amendment, we will experience the Lord's healing in our lives and in our realtionships with others.

"**Lord, have mercy . . .**" In order that this prayer may not be simply routine and that we may experience the Lord's healing, it is helpful to know when these words were spoken. They come from the lips of blind Bartimaeus of whom we read in the Gospel. One day, when he was sitting by the wayside, Jesus and a crowd of people were coming toward him. He inquired from the people as to who was speaking to them. He was told it was Jesus. He became excited because he must have heard about Jesus and about the love that he had for the poor and needy and about the many people he cured. Since he also needed the Lord's healing, he cried aloud, "Jesus, Son of David, have pity on me!" He kept on calling until Jesus asked the people to bring him to him. When he asked, "What do you want me to do for you?" Bartimaeus answered: "Master, that I may see again." Jesus responded, "Go! Your faith has healed you."

In the liturgy we have the same Jesus who healed Bartimaeus and so many others. We have the same Jesus who loves us, wants to help us, wants to heal us. However, in order that our prayer – "Lord, have mercy. Christ, have mercy. Lord, have mercy." – may not be mere words and that we may experience the Lord's power, let us cry out to him with some specific need. If we cry out to him with faith and confidence, he will answer us as he answered Bartimaeus.

The readings and the homily. After reading the Gospel, the priest kisses the page of the Gospel and silently says: "May the words of the Gospel wipe away our sins." The readings and the homily have power to save, to heal, to wipe away our sins because they are the words of God. Through the ministry of the lector and priest, Christ himself proclaims the Good News of the readings, the inspired words of the Holy Spirit, and through the priest he preaches (*Const. S.L.*, 7,33). God's word is always a call to us to be forgiven and saved and to respond to that word through conversion.

In order to experience the Lord's working in our lives, we must be conscious of the truth that it is Christ himself who speaks to us through the readings and homily; with faith, we must listen with an attitude of "We want to hear everything that the Lord wants to tell us today." With such an attitude, as we listen to the Lord week after week, month after month, we will see how our hearts will burn within us and the words will have an effect on our lives. Even though we all hear the same words, the Spirit of God adjusts them to our individual lives.

Preparation of the gifts. We should always bring a gift to the Mass – the gift of ourselves; for in the Mass we offer to the Father not only Christ but also ourselves in union with Christ. On Sundays a collection is taken up. The meaning of this is that, since all we have is due to the goodness of God, in gratitude we give to him, through his Church, a gift in the form of money. But more basically ought it to express that we want to offer ourselves, or at least part of ourselves, on that collection plate. The collection plate is brought to the altar, signifying that we put the offering of ourselves on the paten.

The offering of ourselves is necessary for a meaningful participation in the liturgy. It is better to be specific rather than general in our offering; in this way we will put more into the Mass and receive greater benefit. Furthermore, it is better to offer only one or two things of our life in every Mass, because sincere giving of oneself, even to the Lord, is not easy. Let us offer not only the good and positive things in our life, but also the difficult and negative things; for example, our difficulty with inconsiderateness, envy, jealousy; our difficulty with drinking, smoking, overeating; our temptations and our sins against which we are struggling so much. The Lord died on the cross in order to help us in every phase of our life, hence, he wants us to give him all of our concerns.

The priest then pours wine and water into the chalice. The wine symbolizes the divinity of Christ; the water, our humanity. Doing this, the priest prays: "By the mystery of this water and wine may we come to share in the divinity of Christ, who humbled himself to share in our humanity." We ask that we might become like unto Christ as he became like unto us. This is a small action, but there is so much meaning to it. If we will but offer ourselves, "put ourselves" into the chalice, sincerely asking the Lord to change us, we will experience him in our lives.

Consecration. Before saying the words of consecration the priest extends his hands over the gifts. The symbolism of this is that the priest prays for the Holy Spirit to be present and to change the bread and wine into the body and blood of Christ.

It will also be beneficial to know the following from the Old Testament, namely, that when the high priest offered sacrifice for the sins of the Israelites, two unblemished animals were brought to him. In the same manner, as the priest does in the Mass, he extended his hands over one of the animals, signifying that he was putting all the sins of the Israelites upon that animal. The animal was then set free, but the other innocent one was killed and offered to God as a holocaust for the sins of the people. When Jesus came upon the earth, taking upon himself our human nature, all our sins were put upon him. We were set free, but the innocent Lamb of God was put to death and offered to the Father for our salvation.

Christ continues to offer himself as a Victim for salvation and forgiveness of sins. We see this very clearly in the words of consecration: ". . . this is my body, which will be given up for you . . . this is the cup of my blood of the new and everlasting covenant. It will be shed for you and for all so that sins may be forgiven. Do this in memory of me." Thus, Christ wants us to offer the eucharistic sacrifice in order that we would not forget what he did for us and continues to do.

What happened to the offering we made of ourselves on the paten and in the chalice? Christ is pleased with our offering, takes it unto himself and says: "This is mine, for you have given it to me," and in that aspect of our life which we have offered to him, he helps us to become more like unto himself and gives us his grace and himself in Holy Communion in order to live a more Christlike life. The positive and good things we offered to him, he purifies and makes better; the negative and difficult things, he helps us to bear, struggle against, overcome.

The gradual offering of ourselves, and ultimately of our whole life, ought to mean: "Lord, may your will be done in my life." In this way, "little by little," as we offer ourselves in every Mass, we "pass over" from self to God; in this way, "little by little," we are being "more and more saved": Christ continues to save us with our cooperation.

Holy Communion. Have we ever noticed how frequently the liturgy reminds us of our sinfulness and weakness, as we come closer to the time of receiving Jesus Christ in Holy Communion? For example: "forgive us our trespasses . . . lead us not into temptation, but deliver us from evil"; "keep us free from sin and protect us from all anxiety"; "look not on our sins"; "This is the Lamb of God who takes away the sins of the world"; "Lord, I am not worthy to receive you, but only say the word and I shall be healed." These reminders are made not to discourage us but to help us, for the more we realize our need of the Savior, and the more we realize how much the Lord desires to come to us and to help us, the more will we benefit from the Mass and Holy Communion.

Before we come to receive Christ in Holy Communion, we ourselves tell him the truth: "Lord, I am not worthy to receive you . . ." And, in truth, we are not worthy to receive him. But even though we tell him that we are not worthy to receive him, nonetheless, we know how much he loves us, how much he desires to come into our hearts and into our lives, how much he desires to help us, so with faith and confidence we come to him, saying, "but only say the word and I shall be healed."

Hence, when we receive him in Holy Communion, let us tell him of some specific need of ours, that he may "say the word" as he did to Bartimaeus, and we shall be healed or receive that for whatever we asked.

Finally, by the prayers which the priest recites before receiving Holy Communion, we see what Christ wants to do in our lives. He prays: "Lord Jesus Christ, Son of the Living God, by the will of the Father and the work of the Holy Spirit your death brought life to the world. By your holy body and blood *free me from all my sins, and from every evil. Keep me faithful to your teaching, and never let me be parted from you.*" "Lord Jesus Christ, with faith in your love and mercy I eat your body and drink your blood. *Let it not bring me condemnation, but health in mind and body.*" And when he purifies the sacred vessels, he prays: "Lord, may I receive these gifts in purity of heart. *May they bring me healing and strength, now and for ever.*"

If we shall participate in the Eucharist in this manner, we shall see how the Lord will act in our lives. The more we put of ourselves into the Eucharist, the more will we receive from the Eucharist; the more we give ourselves to the Lord, the more will he give himself to us.

EPILOGUE

I would like to end this presentation of the Eucharist by quoting from the Epilogue of the book, *This Is Love*, by Rev. M. Raymond, O.C.S.O., who wrote the book to help people "get more out the Mass":

> Dear God, I beg you to allow all who read this book to come to the realization that Mass is not something but Someone; that it is your only Son in whom they live and move and have their being, "through whom, with whom, and in whom" they were born and are kept breathing to give you "all honor and glory." Let them realize that Mass, as a liturgical celebration, is an action that has beginning and end, but that Mass, as a life action, goes on after the liturgical celebration is over; and that it is in this life action that they show precisely what they got out of the liturgical action.
>
> Dear God I want them all to be happy, to be joy-filled, in time as well as for eternity. So won't you let them know that they are members

of your only Son's Mystical Body? Hence, they can offer Mass "in him" daily, hourly, every single moment. If they realize that, God, life can hold no real problem for them; no hour of the day or night can be empty; nor any split second of time, sterile. For no matter what you allow to come their way, they will recognize it as something to be offered as wheat, water, and wine; something to be "transubstantiated."

How simple that will make all living for them, God. How readily they will learn how to become more and more holy. For once they take everything in life as "matter" for their Mass, they really have acquired the "mind of Christ" to which St. Paul exhorted all to aspire; for they will see everything as your will. Then they will live in obedience; or better still, in love; for obedience is love in action. Once they acquire that orientation, God, they will have the very courage of Christ to do your will and share in his very power to accomplish it; for they will truly live "in Christ Jesus." Thus life will have become for them what I know you planned it to be for all us humans: a divine romance – a love affair betwen you and ourselves.

What complaint can anyone harbor in his mind or heart, God, no matter what disappointments, contradictions, failures, frustrations, and even defeats come their way, once they acquire the habit of offering themselves as victims "in Christ Jesus" every morning of their lives? Suffering will be felt. But it will never sadden, far less sour them; for they will know that they have offered themselves as victims in this morning's Mass, and that they will need wheat and wine and water for tomorrow's Mass.

The beauty of it all is, dear God, that they will come to recognize the fact that whatever eventuates in their lives comes to them from your hands – and that you will never hand them anything that is not for your glory and their own good. Such realization will have them doing what Paul wanted his contemporaries to do: recognize every seeming folly, apparent contradiction, and real stumbling block as "the power of God and the wisdom of God." They will live by faith and never be surprised by your often surprising ways. You will use them, as you use your closest friends: in ways they never expected to be used; and they will rejoice in their hearts that they are not only being used by God but being of some use to God. When things are at their worst, humanly speaking, these people will be saying in their hearts what they said with their minds and lips in morning Mass: "mindful not only of the blessed Passion . . . but also of the Resurrection and Ascension." Then, like Christ, they will "endure the cross *because of the joy* set before them."

Dear God, do simplify life and living for them by allowing them to appreciate Mass. Let them see that the host in today's Mass yielded its substance so that your Son might be present among us in sacramental and sacrificial form. But that for tomorrow's Mass . . . another host (will be needed). Then they will see that today's joys, sorrows, successes, and failures can serve as "wheat, water, and wine" for today's living of their Mass, but that for tomorrow's living of the same they will need different failures, successes, sorrows, and joys. Thus they will be along from day to day making Mass their life and their lives Mass; spiraling up ever closer and closer to you and your Christ. The simplificaiton will sublimate to this: for his Sacrifice Christ needed his own flesh and blood; for their "Sacrifice" they need nothing more. They need but hold themselves out to you and say: "This is your Body, This, your Blood." You will take them and "transubstantiate" them. Let them live that way, God, and their every heartbeat will go on saying the same thing over and over again without repeating itself once. It will be saying: "My God I love you. I am all yours. Take me, and make me ever more like unto yourse.f" It will never repeat itself, God for each new heartbeat will be newer, greater, more generous love. That, dear God, is the message of the Mass, as I hear it (pp. 148-50).